Able is on the Table

Word Play

Happy Birthday

Mable

Artwork & Story By: AJ Crigler

Able is on the Table

By: A J Crigler

Able is on the Table

Artwork and story by: A J Crigler

StoryTime Publications
P.O. Box 1644
Miamisburg, OH 45343-1644

ISBN-13: 978-0615990828
ISBN-10: 0615990827

This book was printed in the United States of America.

To order additional copies of this book, contact: AJ Crigler at

email: ajcstorytimepublications@aol.com

Able is on the Table

By: A J Crigler

Come my friends and listen to

this tale if you are able.

Come one and all and lend an ear,

to hear this colorful fable.

This fable is about a flashy pig,

who was so called Mable.

She was such a barnyard diva,

dressed in skins and sable.

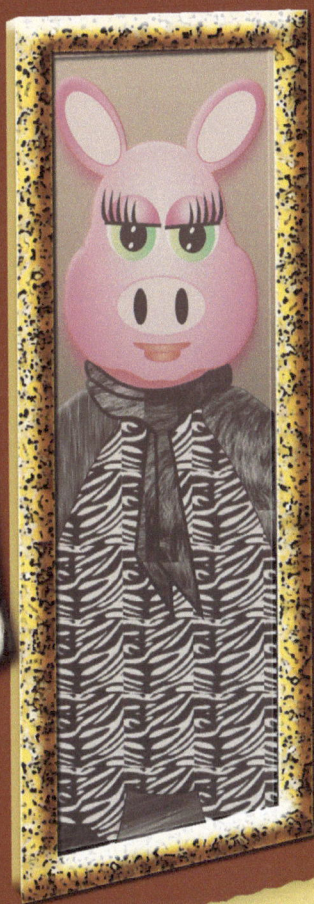

7

She had a sable hat

and a sable tote.

She had two sable boots

that matched her sable coat.

The animals thought she was strange

and did not want to be friends.

She made them all uncomfortable,

because she dressed in skins.

11

"I am so much better," said Mable,

"than those pigs in mud."

One day they laid a trap for her

and she tripped and made a big thud.

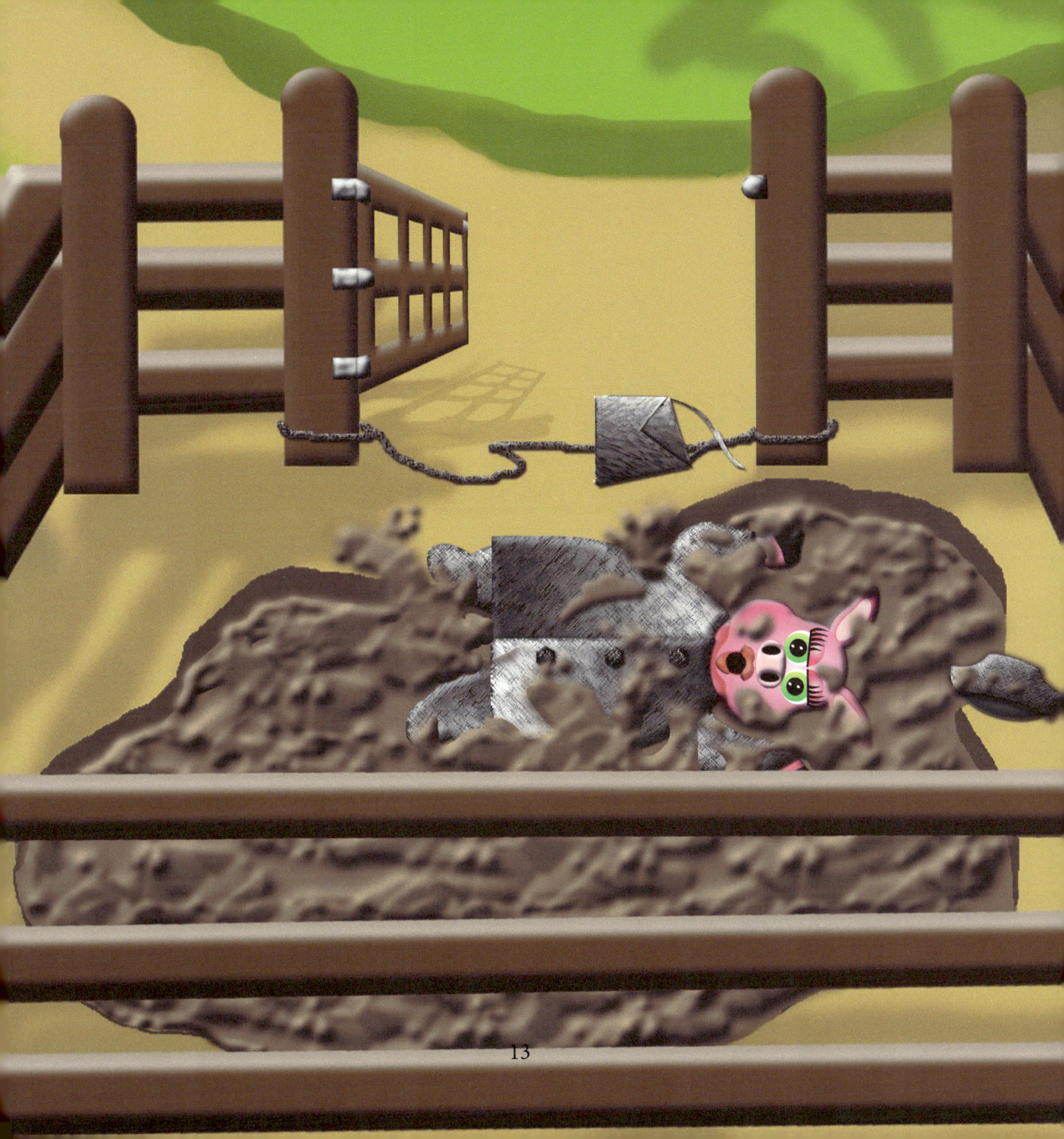

"I knew you were all unsuitable,"

said Mable covered in wet dirt.

"You are all made for the stable,"

as she limped away filthy and hurt.

Mable washed her sable

and hung it out to dry,

but the heaviness broke the cable

and that made Mable cry.

They all laughed at Mable,

in her current muddle.

In anger she gathered up her clothes

and dumped them all in the puddle.

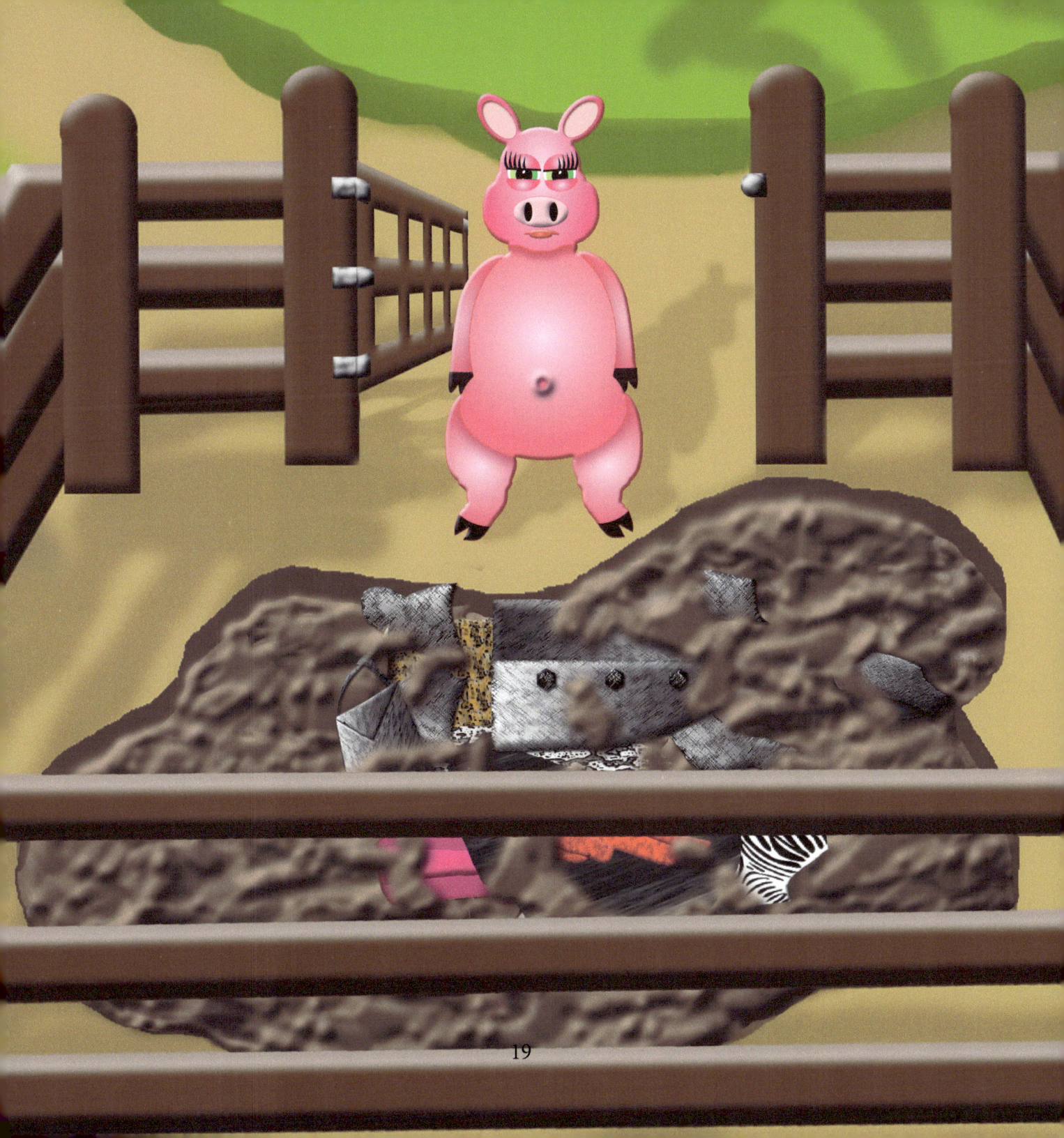

Instead of getting even

Mable prepared a beautiful table,

of all the favorite foods

for everyone in the stable.

They all had a wonderful feast

under the barnyard gable.

She prepared a feast so fine,

they gave thanks around the table.

Mable missed her sable,

every now and then,

but this is much much better,

because she now has kin.

Happy Birthday

Mable

The End

29

Able is on the Table

Able is on the Table (*AIOTT*) is a word play story about a pig who loved to wear fine clothes. Unfortunately the clothes were made of furs and skins that offended all of her friends. The word play for the day is words that end in or contain **A-B-L-E**. It is a learning experience for children 6-12 and also some adults.

In writing *(AIOTT)* I had to find a way to work all the able words into the poem/story. I could see the pictures in my head, but making them come to life would take more than a thought. Writing and illustrating is something that makes me happy. It is exciting when the work is complete. Able... is a fictional fantasy and I hope everyone will enjoy *Able is on the Table* as much as I did creating it.

Reading is essential to life.

Story Time Publications

www.ingramcontent.com/pod-product-compliance
Lightning Source LLC
Chambersburg PA
CBHW041553040426
42447CB00002B/171